Shape and Space

Activities for children with mathematical learning difficulties

Mel Lever

David Fulton Publishers
London

David Fulton Publishers Ltd
The Chiswick Centre, 414 Chiswick High Road, London W4 5TF

www.fultonpublishers.co.uk

David Fulton Publishers is a division of Granada Learning Limited, part of the Granada Media Group.

First published in 2003

10 9 8 7 6 5 4 3 2 1

British Library Cataloguing in Publication Data
A catalogue record for this book is available from the British Library.

ISBN 1-84346-949-1

Designed and typeset by Kenneth Burnley, Wirral, Cheshire
Cover design by Phil Barker
Printed and bound in Great Britain by Thanet Press Limited, Margate, Kent

Shape and Space

Contents

Foreword

Mel Lever is an inspirational teacher of mathematics because she can teach maths to children who don't understand it and don't like it. She contrasts with other gifted maths teachers who can teach maths to children who are good at it. Since there seem to be more pupils who find maths challenging, Mel's ability to break concepts down and to find a creative way of making them accessible is of huge importance.

Mel teaches at Fairley House School, a specialist school for pupils with specific learning difficulties. She teaches maths on a daily basis and, as Maths and Key Stage 2 Coordinator, offers advice and ideas to colleagues. She is also someone who continues to learn and is always ready to take on board new ideas offered by others. She gives workshops to parents on helping children to overcome mathematical difficulties and is in great demand on the lecture circuit for teachers. This set of books means that a wider audience of parents and teachers can be inspired by her ideas.

Mel has studied the teaching of maths for many years and is very familiar with research in the area, particularly into mathematical difficulties. However, she has always chosen to go beyond the theory and to address the vital question: 'So what shall we do about it?' This is what makes her books so helpful; they give parents and teachers practical ideas they can use. Mel addresses the question of the types of difficulty encountered, then moves on to overcoming the difficulty.

At a recent maths workshop for governors, a governor commented, 'I wish Mel had taught me maths when I was at school'. I can only echo that sentiment and urge the reader of these books to enjoy learning from Mel how to teach maths to children who struggle and lag behind.

Jackie Murray
Principal and Educational Psychologist
Fairley House School

Introduction to the Series

Introduction

There are many children who, despite dedicated teachers, the introduction of the National Numeracy Strategy, wonderful books, and an abundance of maths equipment, still do not enjoy or understand mathematics.

We should focus on the two words 'enjoy' and 'understand' because I feel that unless children enjoy their maths, they are unlikely to fully understand it. Children may appear to be functioning reasonably and be achieving set goals, but I am sure that many children could achieve more if they had a 'fun time' with their maths.

I teach dyslexic and dyspraxic children at Fairley House School in London, many of whom have difficulties in understanding maths concepts and functioning mathematically. Over the years I have had to develop ways of interesting these children and helping them to learn. I have diagnosed their difficulties and set about changing my teaching, and that of others, so that maths could be presented to the children in a meaningful and fun way.

It is worth looking at the field of dyslexia in order to summarise the many ways in which children find learning difficult.

The British Dyslexia Association lists many factors that indicate dyslexia. I have picked out the following as being particularly relevant when trying to understand the mathematical learning difficulties of our children:

- Shows confusion between direction words, e.g. up/down, in/out.
- Has difficulty with sequence, e.g. coloured bead sequence, and, later, days of the week.
- Has inability to remember the label for known objects, e.g. 'table', 'chair'.
- Has difficulty learning nursery rhymes and rhyming words, e.g. 'cat', mat', 'sat'.
- Has particular difficulty with reading and spelling.
- Puts letters and figures the wrong way round.
- Has difficulty remembering tables, alphabet, formulae, etc.
- Still occasionally confuses 'b' and 'd' and words such as 'no/on'.
- Still needs to use fingers or marks on paper to make simple calculations.
- Has poor concentration.
- Has problems processing language at speed.
- Has difficulty telling left from right, order of days of the week, months of the year, etc.
- Has poor sense of direction.

Other relevant points could be added to this list. Many children with dyslexia have difficulty with left and right orientation. Many young dyslexic children need aids for doing any arithmetical computation. Some relinquish these aids at the same developmental stage as would the average child. However, the dyslexic and dyspraxic child may well need these aids for a longer time.

Difficulties in recalling multiplication tables are caused by short-term memory problems and by the inability to easily recognise sequences and patterns, thus removing props that help when memory fails. This leads to difficulties with working at speed to solve mathematical problems or when memorising, not only multiplication facts, but also addition, subtraction and division facts. It also leads to difficulties with telling the time, remembering the days of the week and months of the year.

I can hear many teachers and parents saying, 'My child has some of these problems, but he is not dyslexic. Why concentrate on dyslexia?' The simple answer is that I am not concentrating on dyslexia. I am hoping that, by outlining the above, I will give the reader an idea of the issues I am faced with in my work with dyslexic children. Many children have mathematical learning difficulties for a variety of reasons. Because I have worked with children who have difficulties in many areas of the curriculum and in all areas of mathematics, I have been forced to think of ways to overcome these difficulties. In doing so, I have found ways of interesting all children: the devices, games and methods I have developed have been of interest to children in general and their teachers.

Teachers of maths to children with mathematical learning difficulties are aware that every statement or teaching point needs to be rephrased and produced in a variety of ways, using concrete and pictorial methods, if the child is to make any sense of it. Asking a child to accept a mathematical fact and use it is not always helpful. The child may lack reference points and be unable to latch on to any signpost; he or she may lack any internal visual stimulus.

Teachers are constantly diagnosing the learning of their pupils; they learn how to adapt their teaching in the light of knowledge gained. Thus teachers are instruments of change in a school setting and thence in the wider world. Each teacher has a unique view of the wider educational community in which he or she is involved.

My teaching experience has led to a conviction that much mathematical learning is inhibited through children not being offered a wide enough mathematical vocabulary. This does not mean always *adding words* to the vocabulary; it might often mean *adding meaning* to the words already used by the children.

How the series is organised

The National Numeracy Strategy and Maths Schemes are mostly arranged in the expectation of an ordered, sequential and predictable path of learning. Teachers know that this is not how children learn. Maths is not a narrow subject; it is not just a series of truisms and facts. Maths is about discovery and logic; it is about pattern and shape; it is about order and chaos. Anyone reading that last sentence will have a different view of its meaning. We all have a different way of seeing and understanding the various aspects of mathematics. Some aspects of maths are easy for us to understand, some are not.

I considered arranging this series of books into year order: Years 1 to 6 or 7. I then realised that it is impossible to categorise need in this way. The activities I am suggesting are suitable for children in all these years. The principles concerned are adaptable. There is no lower or upper age limit to their usefulness and interest.

I decided to produce a series of books covering the various aspects of mathematics as followed in schools: number, shape and space, measures and handling data. I have omitted solving problems as a heading as this does not lend itself to a separate section here.

The books give ideas for activities to help children learn. Some ideas are more desk-bound than others. Many ideas involve children moving around. I suggest materials that teachers can produce, and supply photocopiable resources. There is much of the Numeracy Strategy that is not mentioned in these books. I have concentrated on areas where we have found children in need of a more creative approach. The creativity of early years teaching is not in question. I have been involved in bringing more creativity into the teaching of children in Years 3 to 6 especially.

Many of my colleagues also develop material for their maths classes and have been happy to contribute their ideas. Teachers are constantly on the look-out for ideas to help their children learn. Most are generous with sharing their ideas. I hope that this is another forum for discussion and that we shall all learn together.

Acknowledgements

I would like to thank my colleagues at Fairley House for their help with getting this series together. In particular I would like to thank:

- Elizabeth Morrell for her support in setting up the project and for reading through the final draft;
- Jackie Murray for proof reading and giving helpful suggestions for improvement; and
- the following for allowing me to include their ideas:

  Mark Bolton
  Caroline Lillywhite
  Rosena Mentior
  Iona Mitchell
  Denise Mulholland
  Ann Osborn
  Jeanette Platt
  Joanne Tarr
  Veronica Woolvett

James Bentall helped with copying the photographs.

1 Shape and Space: Introduction

Children with mathematical learning difficulties often have problems with learning the names of shapes and remembering their properties. Teachers may well find that they need to return constantly to the teaching programmes for earlier years to practise some of the basic skills and learn the appropriate language.

Dyspraxic children and others who find it hard to hold or manipulate tools may miss some of the practical experiences so necessary for concepts to be internalised. Teachers should help by ensuring that as much practical, supported experience as possible is available to each child. The time given to this will be well spent as it will give the children a reference point for further ideas.

The language of shape in the early years is an everyday language and the Numeracy Strategy emphasises this in the teaching programmes for Reception and Year 1. There are many suggested ideas that are relevant and necessary in the teaching of older children. Let us concentrate on language for a while.

Children who have specific learning difficulties may well have difficulties with receptive and expressive language. They will be receiving help with their language development in special groups, or through a general support system. Mathematics is an area where children can be encouraged to expand their language use through numerous activities. The activities that follow are ones that have worked with the dyslexic and dyspraxic children that I teach. Most are appropriate for children at all ages in the primary school.

2 Memory Training

See the *Number* book for more on memory training. Children need help to learn how to remember. Most children need memory training as part of their usual school routine, some needing this more than others. We can show shapes, help children to copy them, learn their names, label them and do all the many things teachers do to help children understand and remember the concepts.

What we need to do is help the children develop their own methods for remembering shapes and shape names. The following activities will help.

Activity 1

Display a picture of shapes as in Figure 2.1. Ask the children to look at this for one minute, after which they will have to draw the shapes. Discuss the results. Ask children to explain how they remembered the shapes. Some will remember shape names and know how to draw those shapes. Some will remember the number of lines and how they join. Repeat the exercise with another picture of shapes. Revise all the shape names they have used.

Activity 2

Place some 3D shapes on a tray. Place a larger selection of 3D shapes on a table, including shapes similar to the ones on the tray. Cover them up. Show the children the shapes on the tray. Ask them to memorise them. Uncover the shapes on the table and ask the children, in turn, to find a shape the same as one of the shapes on the tray. Discuss the results. How did they remember? Encourage them to use mathematical language.

Activity 3

With children working in pairs, ask the children to define a 2D shape to their partner. The partner has to reproduce the shape or point to it on a paper.

Repeat this exercise with 3D shapes, this time asking one partner to describe the shape and the other to find it.

Further work on definition follows in Chapter 4, Marlon Maths.

RESOURCES

- Sheet of shape pictures
- Tray
- Selection of 3D shapes
- Paper
- Pencils

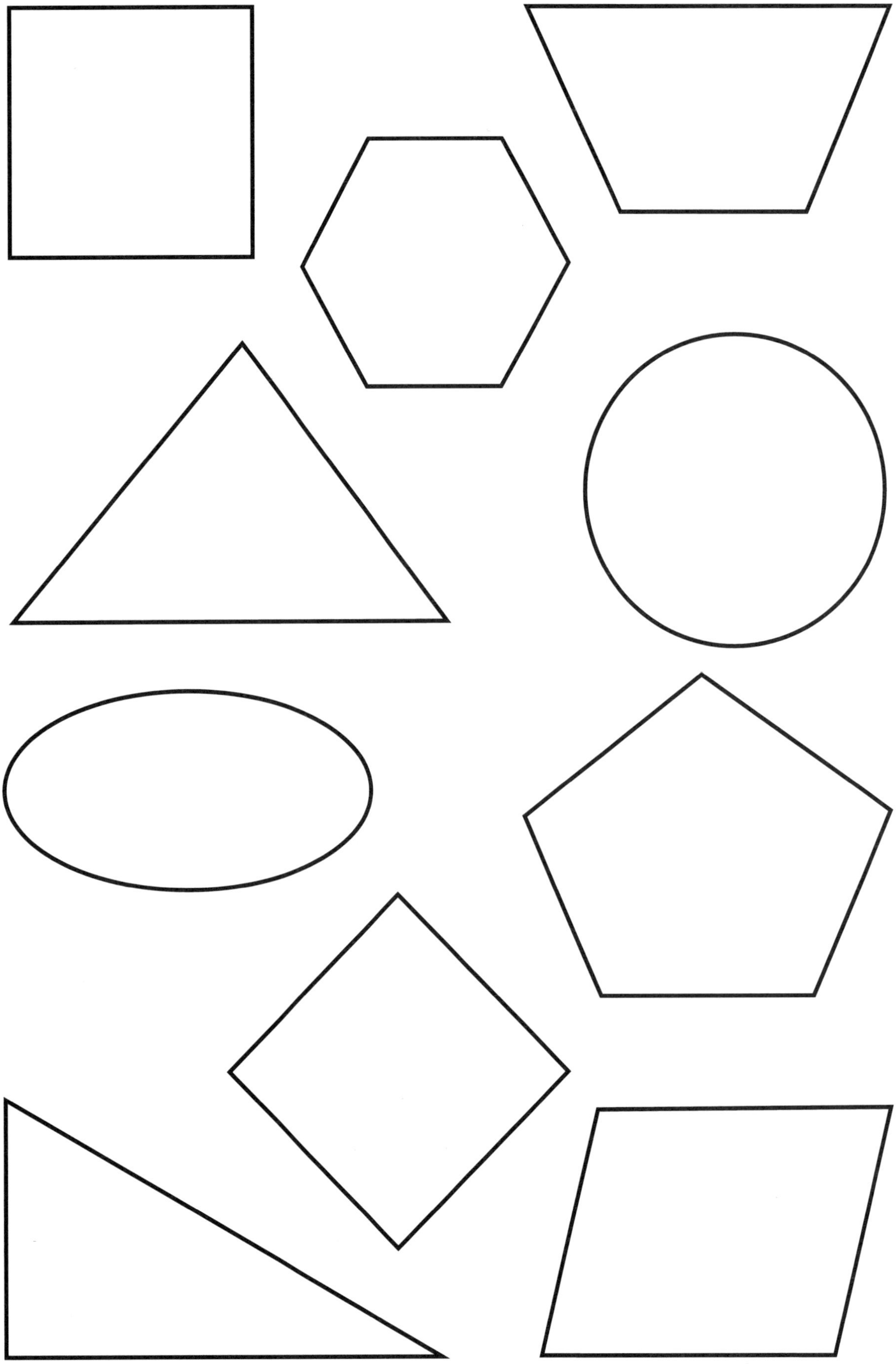

Figure 2.1: A variety of shapes

3 Using Everyday Language to Describe

Children need to develop their skills of observation and description. Teachers can help them through a range of activities. Here are some suggestions.

Activity 1

Children take it in turn to describe an object in the room so that the rest of the class can guess what that object is. They must not say what it is used for. For instance, a pen holder could be described as 'plastic, round, tall'. Obviously the last two words can be interpreted in a variety of ways. The children will soon learn that it is necessary to be more precise. The teacher times how long it takes for the class to guess the object. When everyone has had a go, the winner is the child whose object was found in the shortest time.

Activity 2

Children take it in turn to think of an object in the room. The rest of the class has to ask questions in order to guess what the object is. For instance, children may ask, 'Has it got straight sides?' They may also ask, 'Can you put things in it?' The questions do not have to be mathematical, although mathematical questions will arise naturally.

Activity 3

Draw an object, then describe the drawing to the children in the class, who have to try to reproduce it without seeing it. This is not an easy task, but you can model the way it can be done. If you draw a bus, you may well start your instructions with, 'Draw a vertical line 8 cm long.' With very young children it could be that the precise measurement cannot be used, but you may say, 'Draw a vertical line as long as the short edge of your book.' The use of the word 'vertical' gives children a secure reference point for the rest of their drawing and is also one that is useful for children to use early on.

Knowledge and understanding about 'vertical' and 'horizontal' are vital in mapwork, in art, when drawing diagrams, and in almost every area of the curriculum. The next instruction could be, 'Draw a horizontal line from the left hand edge of your first line upwards for 2 cm.' Alternatively, you could describe the height of this line as being 'as tall as two Multilink cubes' or 'as tall as your smallest finger'. Once you have begun this sort of activity you will soon find out that precise descriptions become necessary and children will become adept at pointing out ambiguity. The same activity can be undertaken at various stages of learning, so that language can include shape names, directions, movements.

Activity 4

Children take it in turn to draw an object. They then describe the drawing to the rest of the class. Everyone has to try to reproduce the drawing without seeing it.

RESOURCES

- Classroom objects
- Paper
- Pencils
- Rulers
- Rubbers

4 Marlon Maths

This is an idea that I came up with some years ago and continue to use whenever appropriate. It arose in a lesson on shape, when I became aware that the children were able to remember some simple shapes, but had a limited understanding of their properties. To ensure that they really thought about this I invented Marlon Maths.

Marlo is a planet. Every so often a visitor from Marlo comes to visit our classroom. The visitor is known as the Marlon. The Marlon often visits when the class has been discussing and learning a new concept. The Marlon can be any visiting adult who can understand the 'rules'; most of the time she is my team teacher. She usually arrives when I need to ensure that those children who are gaining in confidence have acquired the intended degree of understanding, and when some children are having difficulty in understanding, or in expressing their understanding of, the concept.

It is important to ask children to describe what they did in their maths lesson, to ask about the mathematics they used. For many children this is a common experience. For many it is a challenge they can meet. Children with specific learning difficulties do not find this easy. However, the development of their use of mathematical language helps them to clarify their ideas. Discussion and reflection are vital components of the teaching and learning of the dyslexic child. While it is important that they be given the tools to cope with a mathematical curriculum, it is equally important that they be given the opportunity to discuss and describe.

Marlon Maths helps the children refine, broaden and reconstruct their own knowledge. When the Marlon arrives in the classroom she wants to know what the children have been doing. The Marlon has acquired some knowledge of the English language, but there are many words and concepts that she does not know. The children can only find out what these are by talking to her. The first time the Marlon came to my classroom we had been looking at 2D and 3D shapes. I asked the children to tell the Marlon about 2D shapes.

John: '2D shapes are squares, triangles and circles.'

Marlon: 'What is a square?'

John: 'It is a shape with four sides.'

Marlon: 'Is that a square?' (She pointed to a chair that has a top, a bottom, a front and a back.)

John: 'No! A square is something you draw.'

Me: 'Maybe the Marlon can draw it on the board. Would you like to try, Marlon?'

Marlon: 'Yes, please!'

Me: 'Jack, can you start?'

Jack: 'A square has four sides and you can draw it.'

Marlon: 'Like this?' (She drew four non-straight lines, not joined, on the whiteboard.)

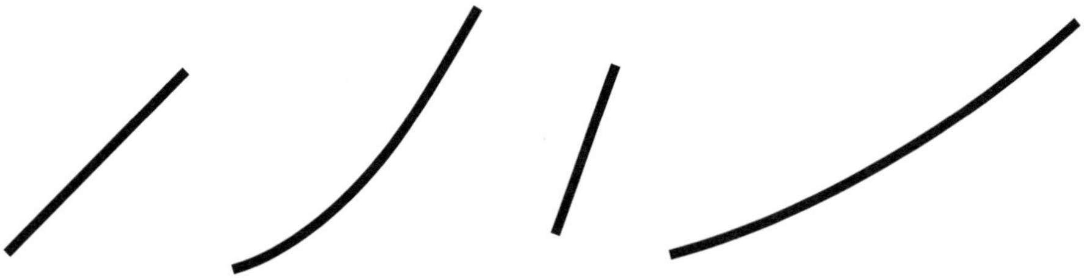

Jack: 'No! They have to all be joined up.'

Marlon: 'Like this?' (She drew the lines again, joining them but not straightening them.)

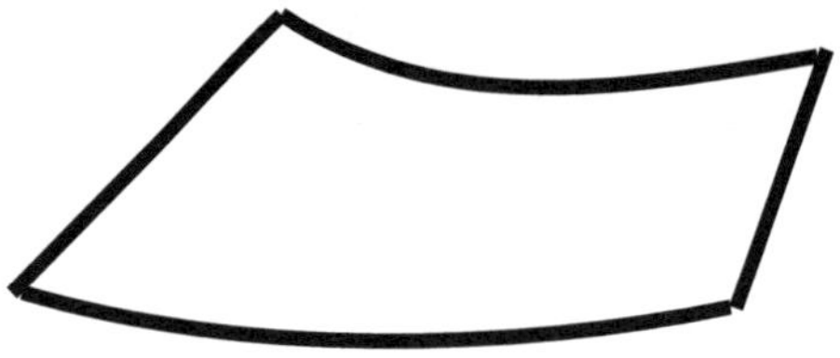

Chorus: 'No!'

Emma: 'The lines have to be straight.'

Marlon: 'How about this?'

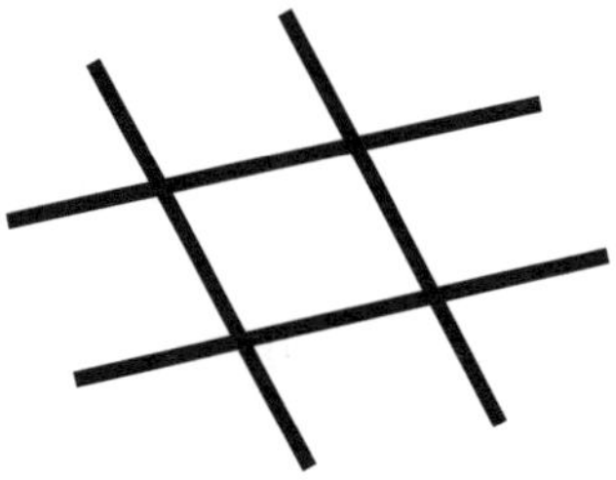

Ben: 'Let me tell you. You need four straight lines and they join up but don't cross each other.'

Marlon: 'Ah! I understand.'

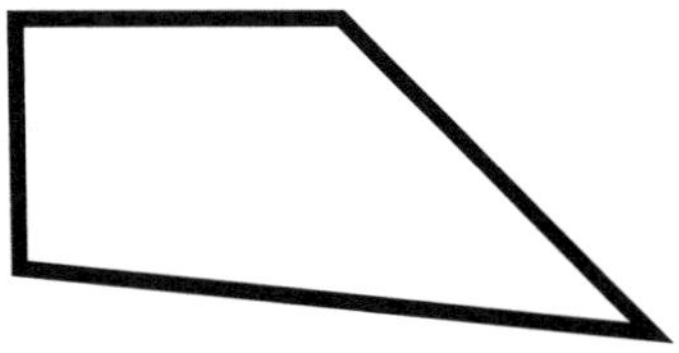

Jack: 'No! Start again. Put your marker on the board. Now draw a straight line across.'

Marlon: 'Like this?'

Jack: 'No! It should be straight.'
Marlon: 'It is straight.'
Me: 'Marlon is right. What do you want her to do?'

(The full transcript of this session can be read in the *Times Educational Supplement* of 15 March 1996.) We continued until the children had used the words 'horizontal' and 'vertical', had thought of angles and corners, and described them and had generally voiced as many concepts as possible.

At the end of the discussion we had a square on the board like this:

I cut out a large paper square and held it up. I asked if this was a square. The children said, 'Yes.' (This was not the moment to go into the fact that if it can be held it is not a square as it is 3D!) I then turned it through 45 degrees.

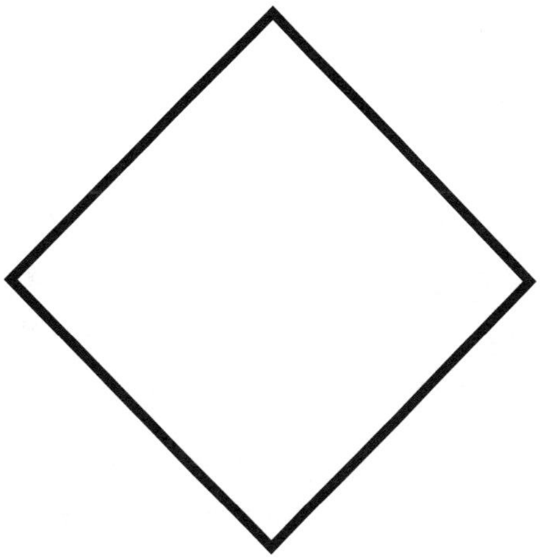

I asked if this was a square. 'No,' chorused most of the children! I turned it back again and then moved it slowly. The children became less sure of their first position. I chose a child and stood him in front of me. 'Is this a boy?' 'Yes.' I then picked him up, turned him through 45 degrees and asked if this was still a boy. 'Yes.' The penny began to drop.

Much discussion ensued and the children were more able after this to think of definitions and to explain their ideas.

This idea can be exploited and expanded to suit the occasion. I use this for all aspects of our maths work. Children have to explain symmetry to the Marlon. Explaining our money system brings in early ideas of decimals. Explaining measurement helps children revise their ideas and discuss or explain the meanings of the terms used.

Marlon Maths can be used at any stage. Ask the children to explain a 100 square to the Marlon. Ask them to explain the meaning of words like add, plus, subtract, divide. Ask them to explain an algorithm. The Marlon (with a few hints from the teacher) knows some words and not others. The teacher knows when to accept a definition and when to press for clarification. Our Marlon has a hat (a card headband with a shiny green circle attached at the front – see Figure 4.1) so we all know when she has arrived. Maybe creatures from other planets can visit classrooms all over the land. We have had a lot of fun with our Marlon and the children have been learning; at the same time the Marlon and I have expanded our knowledge of how children think and understand mathematically. It has helped me to assess how much the children have understood of the lessons we have had and to clarify my own teaching methods.

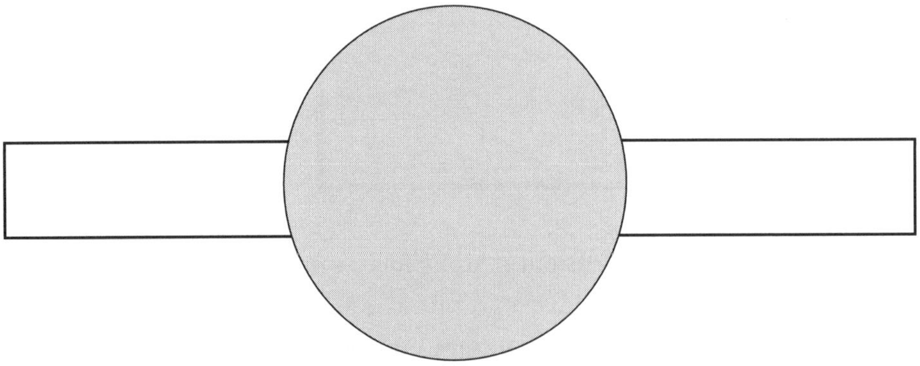

Figure 4.1: Marlon's hat

RESOURCES

- Whiteboard
- Marker pen
- Shapes
- Marlon hat
- Extra adult

5 Language Extension Using Multilink

This is an activity that I have used many times since I was first asked to indulge in it during a Multilink session given by a representative of the firm some 15 or more years ago! It struck me then how useful it was, but it was not until I started teaching dyslexic children that I decided it was a vitally important exercise for these children to undertake.

This takes development of language a step further from what we have been doing with the Marlon. It requires patience and trust. I am not sure if what I am going to describe is exactly what I was taught all those years ago. I have seen variations on it in other publications. Here is what we do.

Activity 1

- Put the children in pairs and ask them to sit back to back. They can sit in the classroom on chairs or on the floor. Due to the noise level, I like them to sit on the floor in the hall!
- Give each child in a pair the same number and colour cubes. For instance, they could have three red, four blue, one black, six yellow. The number you use depends on the age or ability of the children and whether or not they have played before.
- In each pair, one child is A and one is B. Ask A to make a shape by joining all his cubes. When he has done this he must explain to B how to use his squares to replicate the shape. They must not turn round to look or check. Children often need help the first time they do this to know where to begin. It may be necessary for two teachers to demonstrate. The winners are the first pair to complete the exercise correctly.

Activity 2

Ask the children to tell you some of the words they used in their descriptions and write these on the whiteboard. Discuss other words that could be used. Words they need to use are: 'horizontal', 'vertical', 'behind', 'above', 'at the back of', 'in front of', 'to the left', 'to the right', 'at right angles to'. If there is time, ask the children to write down the words themsleves.

Activity 3

Repeat the exercise asking B to make a shape by joining all his cubes. He then has to describe his shape to A. Was the exercise easier for the pair this time?

Activity 4

Change partners. Teachers need to think about how the children are paired. It is sometimes useful to match children by language level. However, pairing one child who has a good knowledge of spatial language with one who has less knowledge can be of benefit to both children. The first will have to be prepared to help someone who is taking longer than expected to follow instructions. He will have to find other ways to describe moves that may seem obvious to him. He will learn empathy! (This can link to work on Emotional Literacy.) The second will hear more relevant language than would have been the case with a less competent child.

I have included these activities as the children are making shapes with the Multilink and describing them. We also use these activities when we have been discussing fractions. Using Multilink to demonstrate fractions and equivalent fractions, we help the children to see fractions as parts of the whole, no matter how or where placed. Rearranging a row of Multilink into an interesting shape helps get this message across.

RESOURCES

- Multilink
- Whiteboard
- Whiteboard marker pen

6 Shapes

Children with specific learning difficulties and those with mathematical learning difficulties have more trouble than ever in remembering shape names. They are more likely to remember the names of shapes if they handle them and define them. Use Photocopiable Sheets A and B to help children define the shapes that they can name.

The following activity helps children to have fun and be creative while learning shape names. It involves planning, sequencing and accuracy.

Activity

- Give each child a sheet of A4 paper divided into sections (Photocopiable Sheet C).
- Show the children some pieces of wrapping paper with repeated patterns on them.
- Ask the children to choose two shapes and two colours and to reproduce these shapes on the paper in a pattern, to make a piece of wrapping paper. They should think of position within the section (see Photocopiable Sheet D).
- Repeat the exercise, this time with A3 paper.
- Ask the children to do a repeating pattern of different triangles – an equilateral, an obtuse and a reflex.
- Extend the above and introduce your own rules. Depending on what the children have been doing, and how far they are taking their understanding and use of the language of shapes, you can help them develop their own patterns.
- Use EXCEL to produce wrapping paper. You can make the grid and the children can design the shapes. Using EXCEL helps dyspraxic children to show their knowledge, exercise their imagination and avoid the drudgery of producing accurate diagrams.

RESOURCES

- Paper
- PC
- Coloured pencils or felt tips
- Rulers
- Protractors
- Photocopiable Sheets A and B

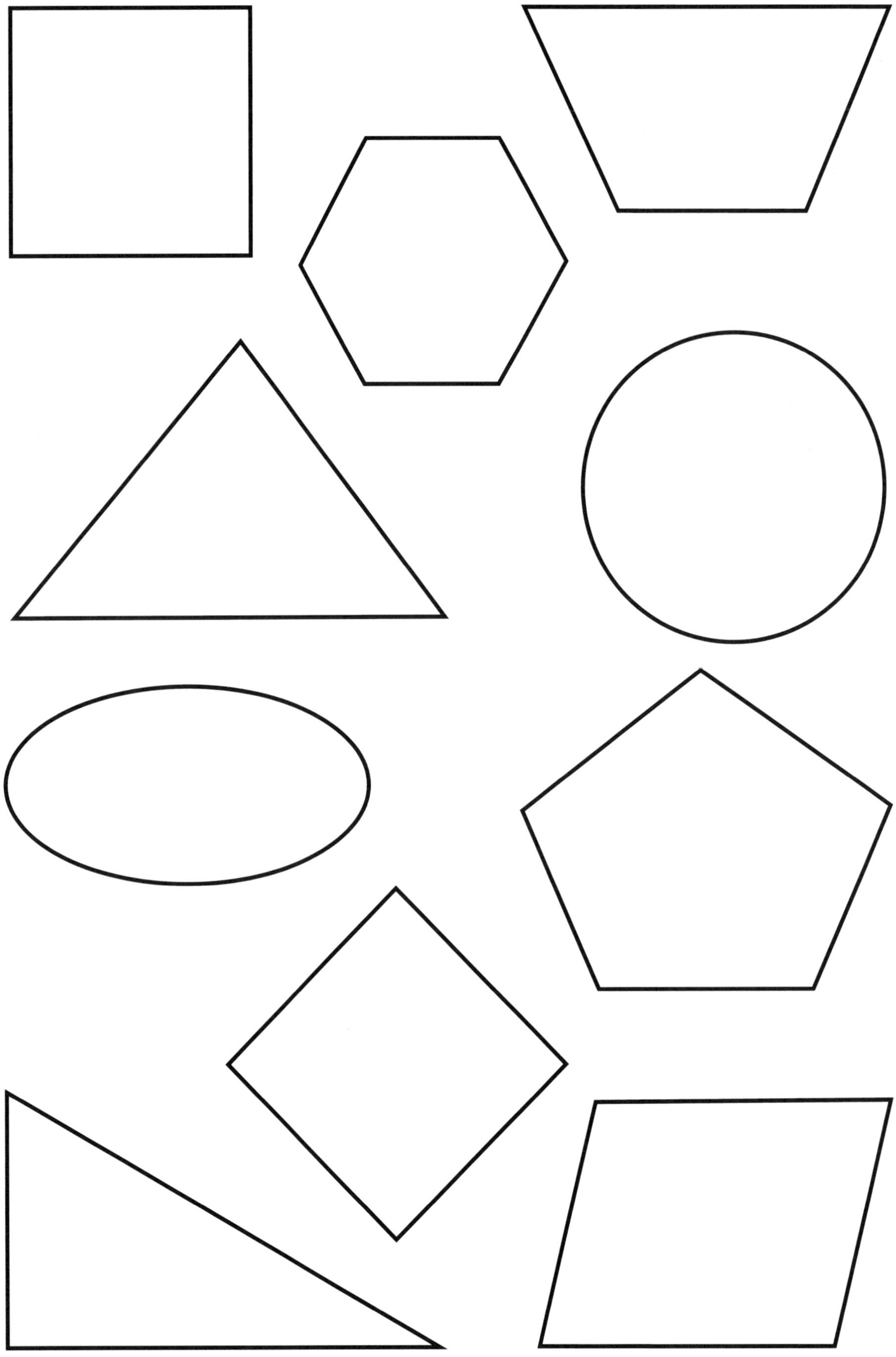

Photocopiable Sheet A

Write the details of the shapes you have made.

Shape	Faces	Edges	Corners

Photocopiable Sheet C

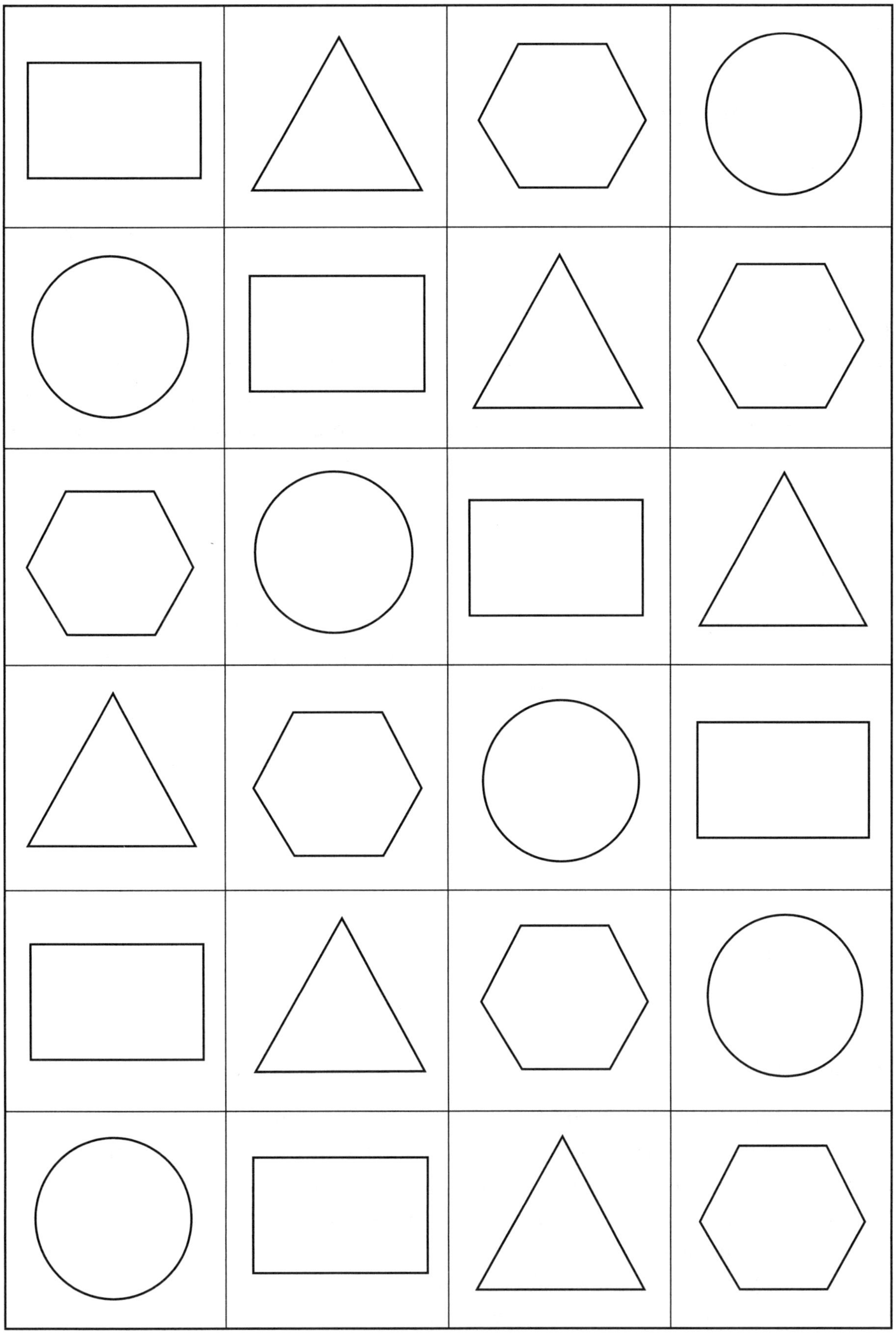

Photocopiable Sheet D

7 Symmetry

I like this aspect of maths: it lends itself to such a lot of creative, fun activities. It fits in well here when we have the opportunity to look at shapes and discuss whether or not they are symmetrical. A lot of comparison and experimentation can take place, looking at geometric 2D shapes. Some children find symmetry difficult to visualise and describe. The following ideas have worked well to help the children see the need for accuracy and to be able to define the concept.

Activity 1

Discuss symmetry and explain to the children that in reflective symmetry each side must be a reflection of the other. Demonstrate this with a series of pictures that can be halved and folded on top of each other.

Activity 2

Ask the children to get into pairs and look at each other's face. Are faces symmetrical? Most children will think they are. Give out one-sided mirrors that are big enough to reflect a whole face and ask the children to take it in turns to put the mirror on their partner's face, resting one edge down the centre of the face. Now ask again if faces are symmetrical. Turn the mirror over to reflect the other side of the face. Did the children see the same 'face' no matter which way the mirror was facing?

Activity 3

Choose a child to stand in front of the class. Is this child symmetrical? By now, some children will doubt it; others will think she is. Find a long mirror and ask the child to stand with the mirror edge stretching from her toes to the top of her head. The teacher will have to hold the mirror. Ask the children if the child looks the same in the mirror reflection and the adjoined side as she did without the mirror. This should generate another lively discussion. Now reflect the other side and ask the same questions as before, adding a question about the two mirror reflections.

Activity 4

Give out lots of pictures of animals, flowers, objects, people. Ask the children to try to decide which ones are symmetrical.

Activity 5

Cut some pictures in half, stick the halves on paper and ask the children to copy them to produce the second half. Emphasise the need to be accurate.

Activity 6

Explain to the children that some things look symmetrical, but that symmetry is an exact word and, in reflective symmetry, both sides must look the same.

RESOURCES

- Symmetrical pictures
- 20 cm square mirrors
- A long mirror
- Pictures of symmetrical objects
- Pencils

8 Symmetry Using Squared Paper

Demonstrate a symmetrical picture on squared paper, showing the line of symmetry (see Photocopiable Sheet E). Revise with the children the facts and concepts pertaining to symmetry. Give children copies of the picture and ask them to fold it down the line of symmetry, demonstrating that each side is, in fact, a reflection of the other. The following activities will help the children to understand the concept and appreciate the need for accuracy.

Activity 1

Give children a copy of Photocopiable Sheet F and ask them to draw in the reflection to produce a symmetrical picture. Ask them what they see now. (They should see a house.) Discuss any errors made. Children need to think about counting squares from the centre line and copying the correct number on the other side. They need to check for the reflection of unfilled shapes.

Activity 2

Do the same as above with Photocopiable Sheet G and ask what the children see. This may well generate different responses, although to me it looks like the top of a robot. Were the children more accurate this time?

Activity 3

Use Photocopiable Sheet H. This is rather more difficult than the ones above as there are no recognisable outcomes. Again, discuss the finished pictures.

Activity 4

Ask the children to work in pairs. Give each child an empty grid (Photocopiable Sheet I) and ask them to make a pattern (half a picture) on one side of the paper. Use one colour only. Swap the sheets and ask the children to complete the second half of this symmetrical picture.

Activity 5

This activity is the same as the last one, but this time allow the children to use three colours. This immediately makes the second part of the task much more difficult as the children need to check position and colour when matching filled-in squares.

Activity 6

Make a grid, using EXCEL, and save it so that the children in your class can access it. Ask the children to work on the computer, making a shape on one side of the grid by filling in the squares. Ask a partner to complete the symmetrical picture by filling in squares on the other side of the line of symmetry. This can be as easy or difficult as you like. You can make the squares any size you feel appropriate. Many children like to do this work on their computers as it saves the effort involved in colouring in a square!

You can get 1 cm squared paper and 2 cm squared paper. These exercises can be done with either size. I tend to start with the larger squares so that children can see results quickly. The larger squares are easier to colour neatly. The smaller squares allow the children to be more creative and to vary the patterns more easily.

RESOURCES

- Squared paper
- Photocopiable Sheets C–G
- Coloured pencils
- PC

Use this grid to make a symmetrical picture.

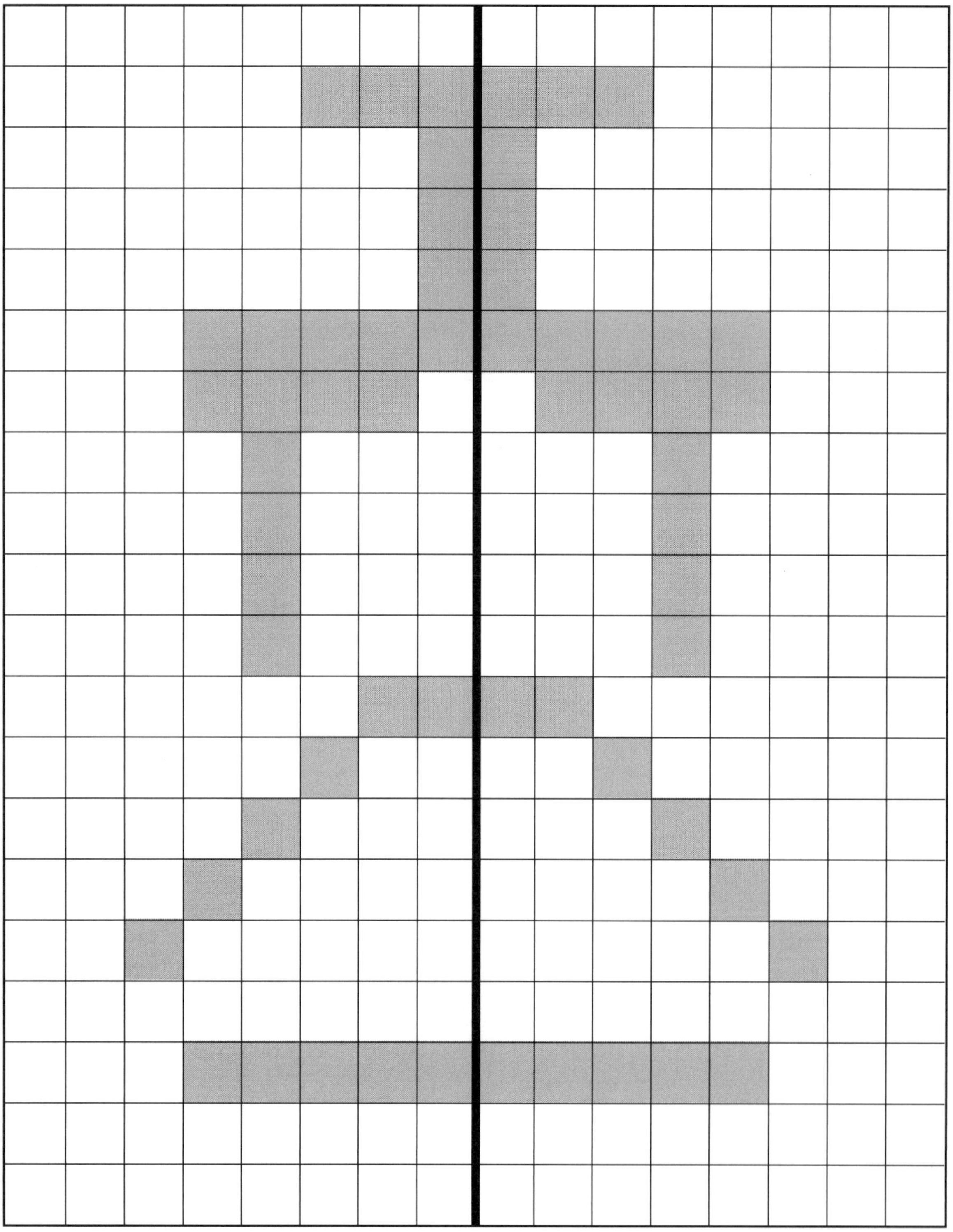

Use this grid to complete the symmetrical picture.

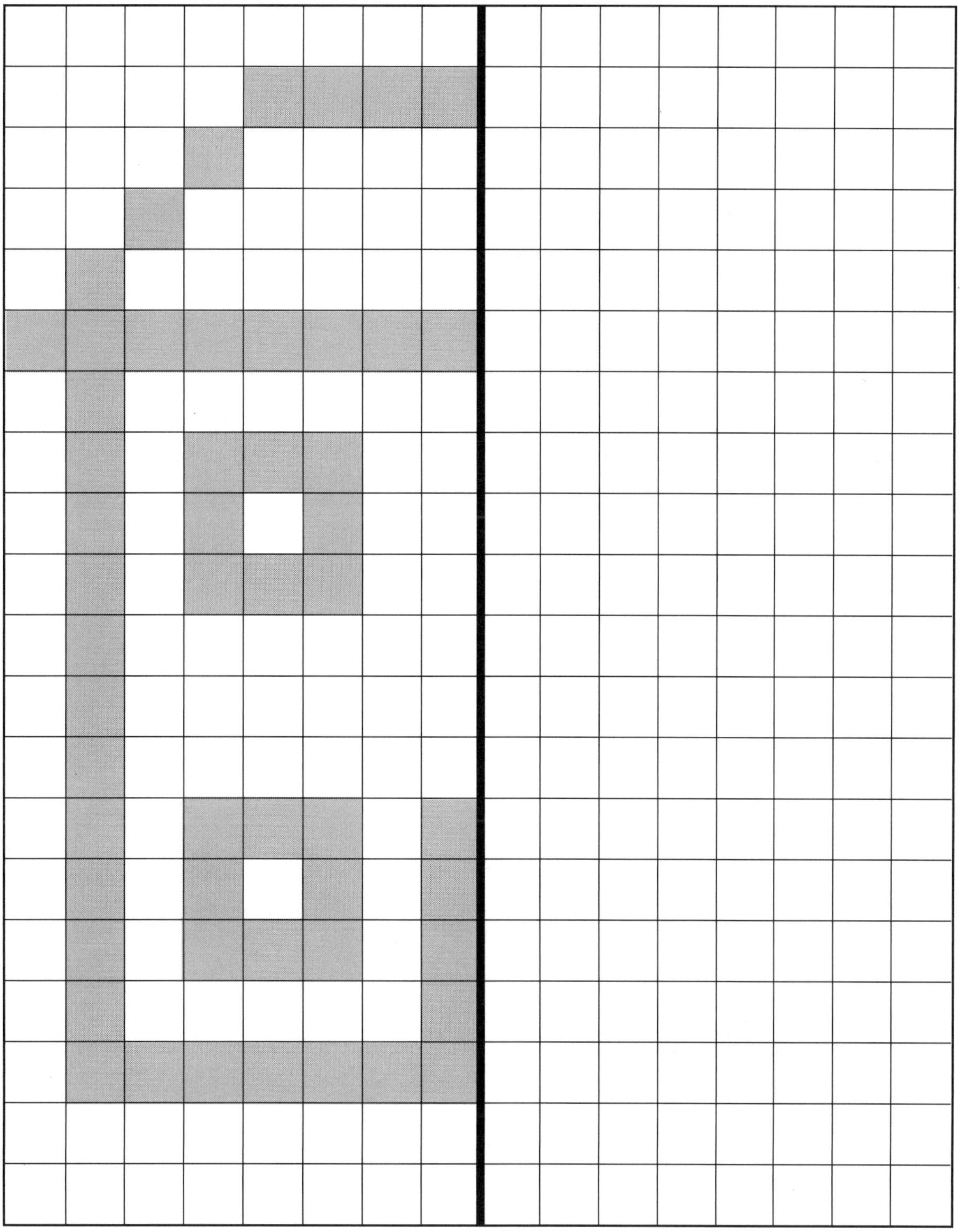

Use this grid to complete the symmetrical picture.

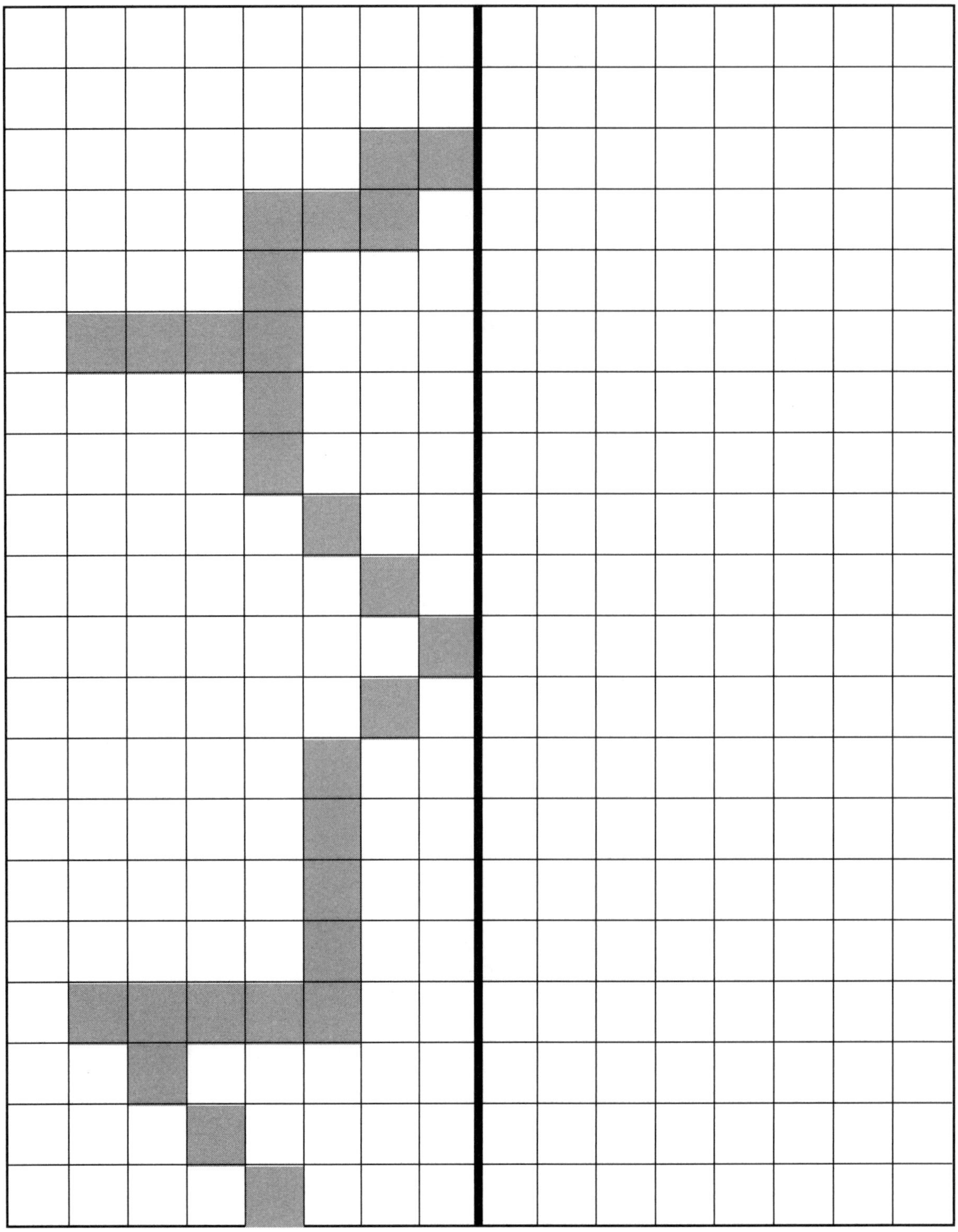

Photocopiable Sheet G

Use this grid to complete the symmetrical picture.

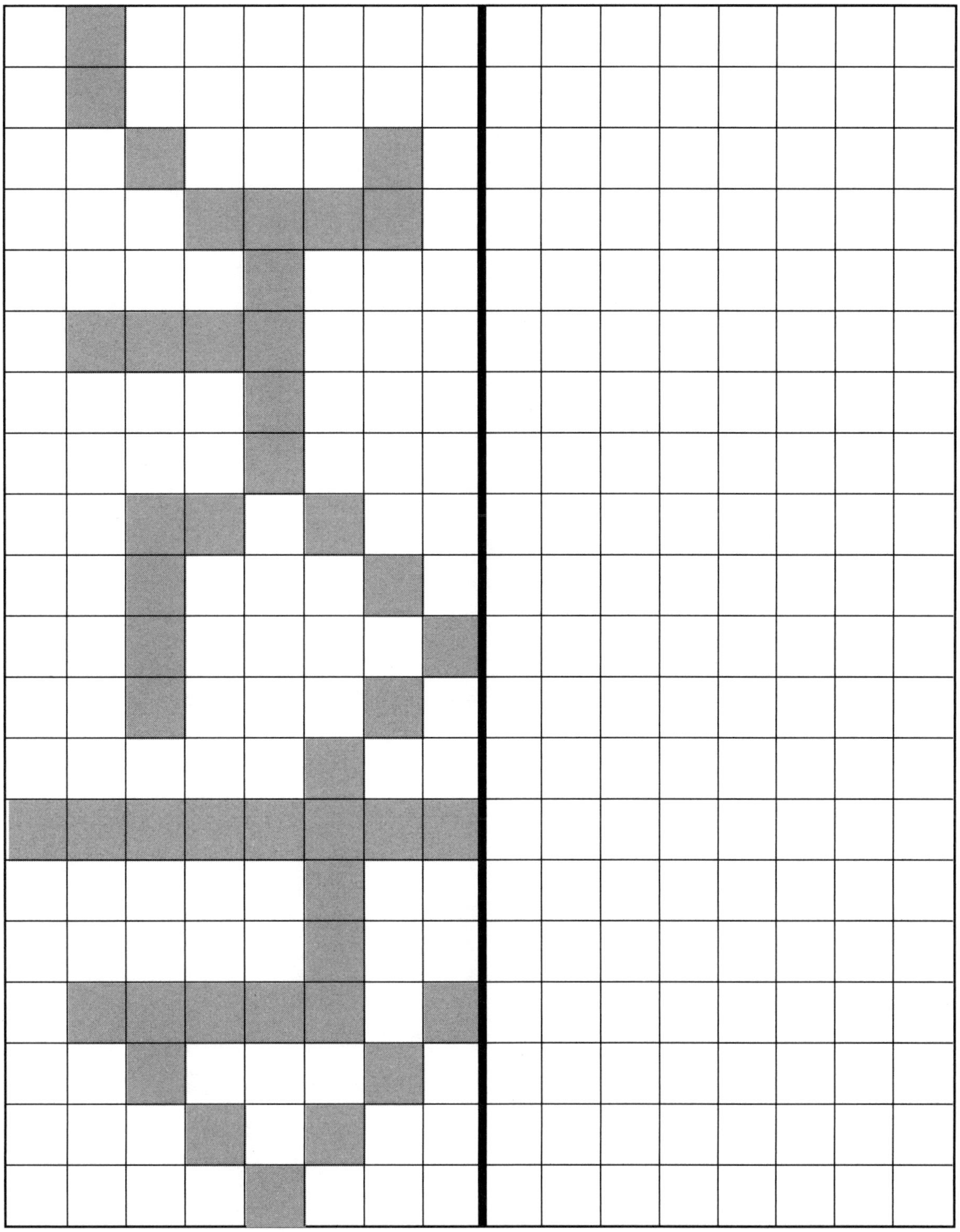

Use this grid to make a symmetrical picture.

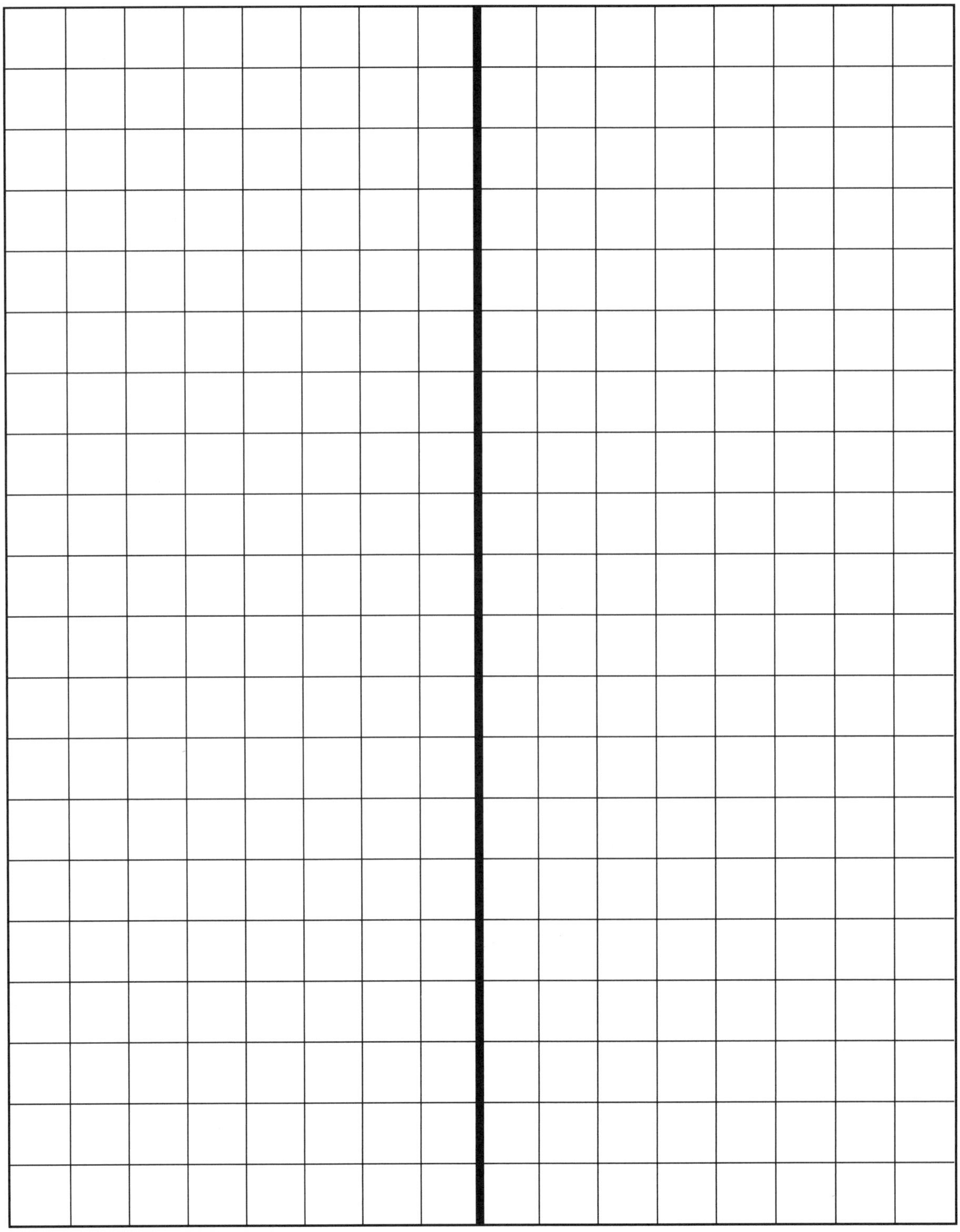

Photocopiable Sheet I

9 Rotational Symmetry

Children can have fun with this, designing circular mats. The following activity gives children scope to use their imagination. It is also a valuable activity for children who have difficulty manipulating concrete materials.

Activity

Give each child a piece of card, a square piece of paper, a drawing pin, a piece of plasticine, sellotape and a strip of card 10 cm long and 1 cm wide.

- ▶ Ask the children to cut out from their piece of card a shape, such as a person, a car, a rabbit.
- ▶ Ask the children to push the plasticine firmly onto the middle of their desk. Place the paper over the plasticine so that the plasticine is in the centre of the paper.
- ▶ Attach one end of the card strip to the cut-out shape, using sellotape, and the other to the drawing pin.
- ▶ Push the drawing pin into the plasticine through the paper.
- ▶ Ask the children to draw round the shape on the end of their strip, holding the shape down so that it does not move, and keeping an eye on the drawing pin so that it does not come out of the paper and plasticine.
- ▶ Ask them to move the shape by rotating the card strip. They should move it so that the card shape does not overlap the drawn shape.
- ▶ They then draw round the card shape again and continue this exercise until they have something that looks like Figures 9.1 or 9.2. (The number of shapes they can draw depends on the size of the outline.)
- ▶ Ask the children to remove the card and drawing pin from their paper and hold it up. They should slowly rotate their picture. Discuss that happens. What did the picture look like before being turned? How does this compare with how it looks now?

RESOURCES

- Pieces of card
- Square pieces of paper
- Drawing pins
- Sellotape
- Strips of card 10 cm long and 1 cm wide
- Pieces of plasticine

Figure 9.1: Rotational symmetry – example 1

Figure 9.2: Rotational symmetry – example 2

10 The Language of Turn and Angle

For many children this is a difficult section of mathematics. Having got the hang of measuring straight lines, and dealing with volume and capacity, many do not find it at all easy to understand how they can measure turn. They need to understand circles before they can understand angles.

The Numeracy Strategy has useful suggestions of activities that help children gain the concepts. There are ideas related to equipment and toys in the classroom, such as clocks, wheels, scissors, windmills, and ideas that can be used in PE. Teachers should refer to the ideas in those early years for help with teaching older children who still have difficulty in understanding this aspect of mathematics.

With our dyslexic and dyspraxic children, the emphasis, as always, has been on moving, on using the whole body. The larger the example, the easier it is for the child to grasp the idea. The following have helped us to teach our children.

Actvity

- Ask the children to stand in a space in the hall. They should shut their eyes, or wear a blindfold, and follow the directions given by the teacher. Directions could be: 'Walk four short steps forward. Turn to your right and walk forward three short steps. Walk backwards six short steps. Imagine which way you are facing and where you are. Open your eyes and check.' Much discussion should ensue. Some children will be surprised. Some will have bumped into each other.
- Discuss the language you used. Can they all understand the words, 'forward', 'backwards', 'turn right'?
- Choose two children to demonstrate. Ask them to stand facing the rest of the class. Ask them to turn round on the spot so that they end up facing the same way that they started. How could we describe what they did in another way? The children should be encouraged to think about clockwise and anticlockwise turns and a whole turn.
- Ask children in turn to imagine a shape on the floor and walk along their shape. Can the other children tell what shape it is? Ask the first child to describe the shape as he or she walks it again. Many children will choose a rectangle or square and thus be able to turn left or right without specifying how far (for the other children will accept this).

- ► Ask the children to imagine a triangle on the floor. Ask them to walk along the sides. Can they describe to another child what they did? What happens at the turn? Can they say 'Turn right' or 'Turn left'? How far did they turn?
- ► Discuss with the children how they might describe angles of turn more exactly. They should see the need for some measurement using standard units. They are now ready to go on to making circles.

Walking in a circle

Following instructions blindfolded

11 Making Circles

What is a circle? Whenever you ask a class of children this question, you will get a lot of fingers in the air and a chorus of replies, 'It goes round and round,' accompanied by circular movements with the finger!

You can use Marlon to encourage the children to define circles more accurately. Even if they do not arrive at the final definition themselves, they will have rehearsed a lot of the language of shape. To encourage them to come to an accurate definition, try the following activities.

Activity 1

Draw an ellipse and a circle and see if the children can explain the difference.

Activity 2

- Draw a circle and say this is the performing ring in a circus. Put the ringmaster in the middle.

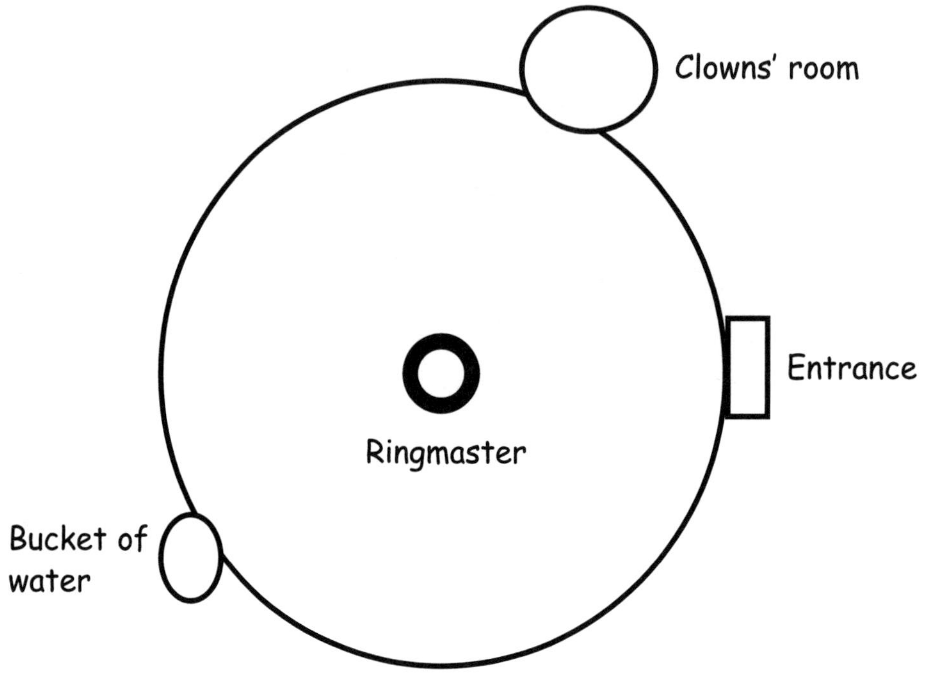

- Mark some key circus points, e.g. bucket of water, clowns' room, entrance.
- Ask the children which point they think the ringmaster could reach the most quickly if he walked to them.
- Give each child a copy of the drawing and ask them to measure the distance from the ringmaster to each of the outer points.
- Agree with them that the distances are the same. What does this tell us about a circle?

You will eventually reach a working definition and can introduce the language that accompanies it: 'circumference', 'radius', 'diameter'.

Activity 3: Make a circus ring

- In a large room (school hall), ask the children to sit at the edge of the room. Choose one child to stand in the centre of the room and give him or her a piece of string, about 3 metres long. Ask the class to think of some way of using this child and the string to make a circle. Prompt them by reminding them of the language of circles that they have used. The circumference is the same distance from the centre no matter where you measure it. Discussion should lead to the following solution:
- The child in the centre (child A) holds one end of the string. Another child (child B) holds the other end and moves as far away from the first child as possible (holding the string comfortably taut). Child B walks round a circle, child A turning on the spot to keep facing him.

Activity 4: Make a smaller circle

Having done the above exercises, the children are now ready to think of angles as turns.

- Give each pair of children a piece of paper, a short piece of string, a lump of plasticine, a pencil and a drawing pin. Ask them to discuss how they could use these to draw a circle. They should eventually find that they can put a small lump of plasticine on their desk and lie the paper on it. They then tie the pencil to one end of the string, put the drawing pin through the other end and put this through the plasticine. Keeping the pencil vertical they can now draw their circle.
- Ask the children to use a ruler to measure the radius at various points on the circumference. How accurate was their circle? Can they think of any way of being accurate? Help them to think of the necessity of being exact in measurements, of using inflexible tools.
- Introduce the compass and explain its use. Ask them to draw circles using a compass. Discuss the different circles. Are any of them the same as anyone else's? What are the variables?
- Give the children a radius and ask them to draw a circle of this radius. Compare. All circles should be the same.
- Give the children a diameter and ask them to draw a circle of this diameter. Discuss how this can be done. Compare end results.

The movement and discussion suggested above will help all children retain the basic concept of a circle and use it to further develop their work.

RESOURCES

- Picture of circus ring
- String
- Paper
- Pencils
- Rulers
- Plasticine
- Drawing pins
- Compasses

12 Further Work on Angles

Once children have had all the practical experience suggested above, they are ready to think about measuring angles of 2D shapes. These angles are measurements of turn – and the children have done a lot of turning!

This is the time when children can be introduced to facts:

- a full turn is 360 degrees;
- a half turn is 180 degrees;
- a quarter turn is 90 degrees – this is also called a right angle.

Show them how this is measured using a protractor.

Display a large circle with the above facts marked on it (Figure 12.1). Hold a thin stick along the radius marked 0 degrees and 360 degrees. Move the stick through an angle of 45 degrees and ask the children to estimate through how many degrees it has moved. Do this with other angles.

Facts relating to 2D shapes will be much easier for the children to understand and use once they have had all this practical experience.

RESOURCES

- Diagram (as in Figure 12.1)
- Stick
- Protractors

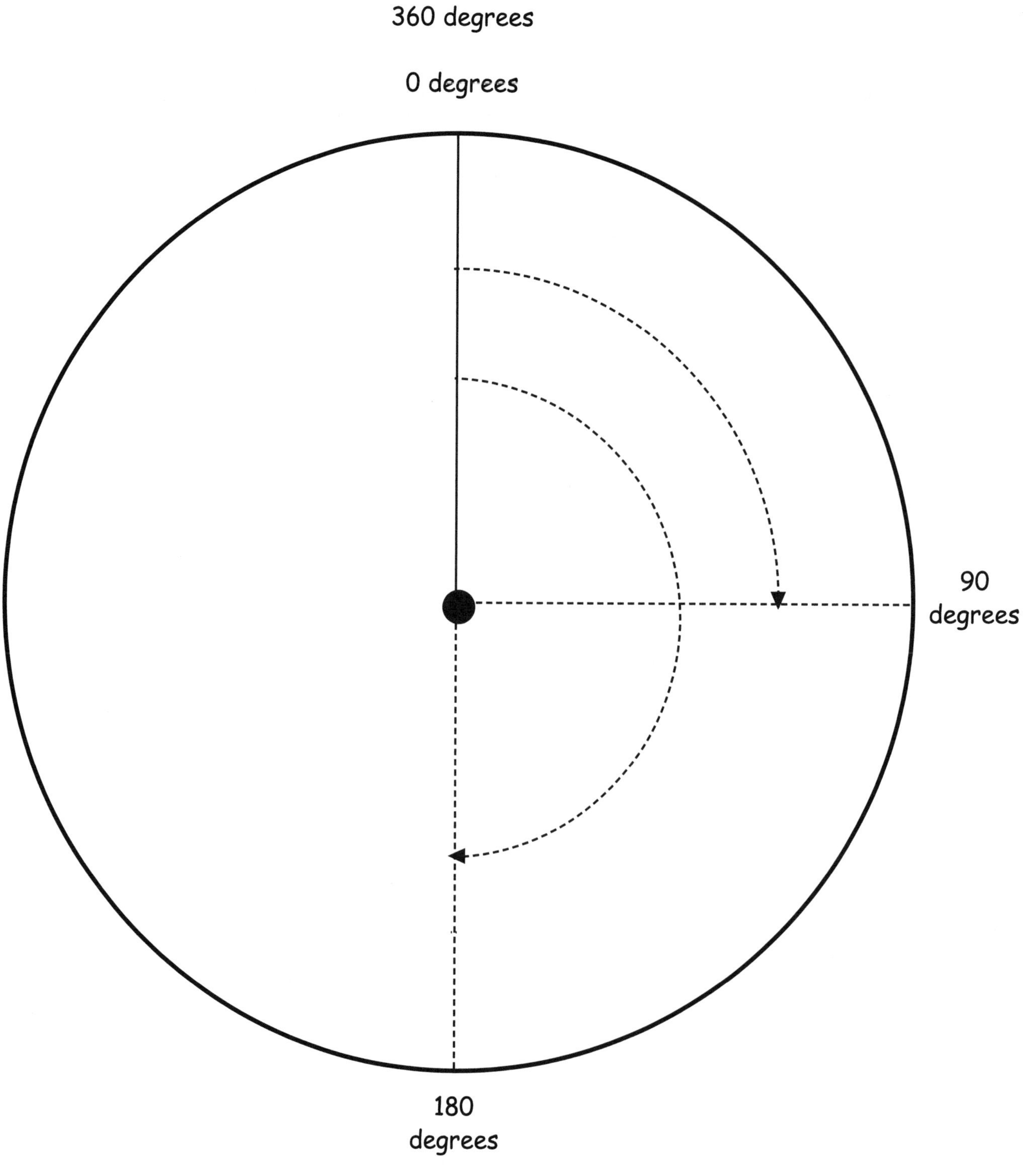

Figure 12.1: How angles are measured

13 Making Turns

This follows on from 'Making Circles' (Chapter 11). It also fits in nicely to work on time (see section in the *Measures* book, pp. 3–19).

Mark a circle in the hall. If the hall is marked for games it might now look like Figure 13.1 (the circle being drawn with chalk or marked with beanbags).

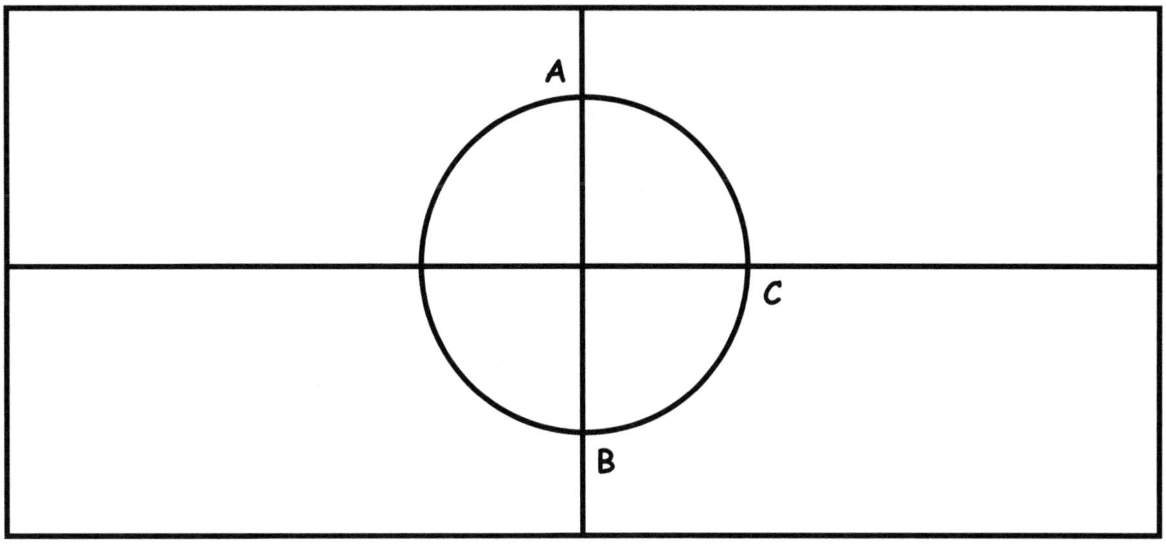

Figure 13.1: Position of the circle marked in the hall

The following activities help the children understand turns and angles through using their bodies and developing their language.

Activity 1

Ask a child to stand at point A on the circle and walk around the circle in a *clockwise* direction until he arrives back at where he started. Discuss the word 'clockwise'. This child has walked around the *whole* circle.

Activity 2

Ask a child to stand at point A and walk clockwise around the circle to point B. How far round the circle has she gone? She has gone *half-way*, and done a *half-turn*.

Activity 3

Ask a child to start at point A and walk around the circle to point C in a clockwise direction. How far has he gone? Relate to time if this is difficult for the children. He has gone quarter of the way, or done a *quarter-turn*.

Activity 4

Repeat all these instructions, sending children in an *anti-clockwise* direction. Start at different points on the circle.

Activity 5

Introduce the word 'angle'. Ask for definitions. Let the children use the floor circle to illustrate what they are saying.

Activity 6

Ask the children how they would measure a circle. How would they measure how far they had moved around a circle?

Activity 7

Illustrate the need for a special way of measuring a turn by asking one child (X) to hold the end of a fairly long pole. Ask another child (Y) to hold the pole half-way along, and a third (Z) to hold the pole at the far end (see Figure 13.2).

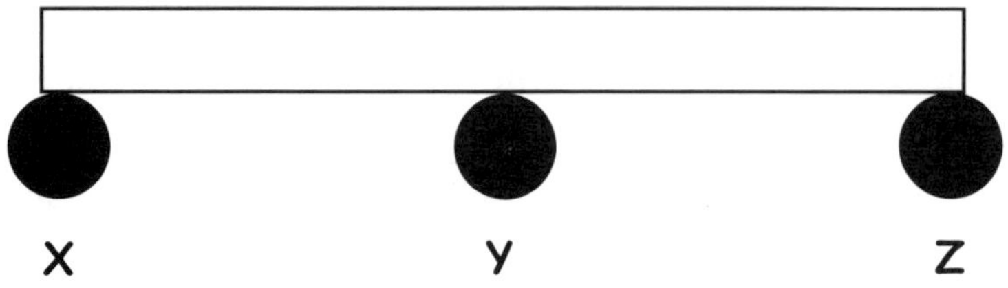

Figure 13.2: Using a pole to measure turns with a child at positions X, Y, Z

- Child X is told to stand in the same spot, turning as children Y and Z move around her. Ask children Y and Z to move very slowly. Stop them after about a quarter move and ask which child has moved the furthest.
- Ask the children how they would measure this. They may decide to measure a straight line from where child Y started out and where he ended up and the same for child Z. The teacher can then ask the children if child X moved further to keep

up with child Z than she did to keep up with child Y. This should generate a lot of lively discussion.

► Explain that what we measure with angles is the turn at the centre, the turn that, in this case, child X has made. It is difficult to measure that on the spot so we measure from a little away from the centre. The distance walked by child Z is further than the distance walked by child Y, but the turn of child X is the same. In fact, it can now be demonstrated that all the children are keeping in the same straight line.

Activity 8

Introduce the protractor and explain that this measures the angle of turn from the centre and, as has been demonstrated, by turning completely around, a circle has been made. The angle is measured from the centre, and the further away from the centre we are the greater the distance between two points, although the turn at the centre remains the same.

RESOURCES

- Chalk or beanbags
- Long pole
- Metre sticks and tape measures
- Set of protractors

14 Points of the Compass

Many children find it difficult to remember the compass points. They are fun to learn through games. The following activity has worked well with dyslexic and dyspraxic children.

Activity

Give four children a word card each: North, South, East and West (Photocopiable Sheet J). (All cards in these activities should be laminated.) Ask North to take up a position in the hall at one of the points marked as in Figure 14.1.

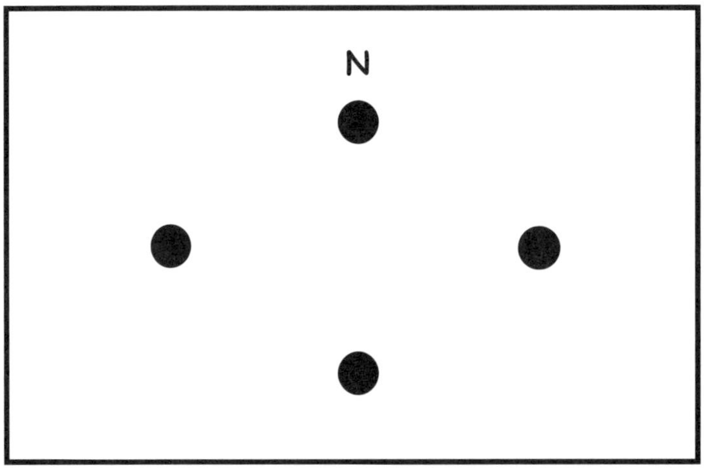

Figure 14.1: Position of compass points in the hall

- Ask the other three children to get into position. This can engender lots of discussion, trial and error, and correction. The four children with cards and the rest of the class will remember the movements.
- Give out four more cards: North East, North West, South East, South West (Photocopiable Sheet K). Ask these children to get into position. This will engender a lot more discussion. Is North East nearer to North than to East? If it belongs to both North and East, how can it be fair to both of them? The class should eventually find a position half-way between the two.
- Explain that it is often easier to use letters instead of whole words to illustrate positions. Hold up N, S, E and W and ask the children to say what they think they stand for.

- Now hand out four more cards: NNE, SSE, NNW, SSW (Photocopiable Sheet L). Ask these children to find a position to stand in. This is a much more difficult move than the others. Deal with NNE first. Ask the child holding the card to use a felt tip to split NNE into two sections, each of which is already in the circle. He or she should eventually, maybe with help from the rest of the class, find North and North East (N and NE). Now he or she can take his or her position in the circle. The rest should find it easier to follow.
- Give out four more cards: ENE, ESE, WNW, WSW (Photocopiable Sheet M). Ask the children to find a position to stand in. Again, you will need to need to help one child to find a position first. Take ENE and ask the child holding it to use a felt tip to split it into two sections, each of which is already in the circle. He or she will eventually find E and NE and place himself or herself between these two positions. The others should follow.

This series of activities can be repeated often. The children find it fun trying to be first to find their place. They work in a large space and can move around. The language is practised and remembered. Children learn to give directions as they help each other.

These activities can also be done as a team exercise. Points can be given for being the first to find the correct space.

RESOURCES

- Points of the compass cards (Photocopiable Sheets J to M)

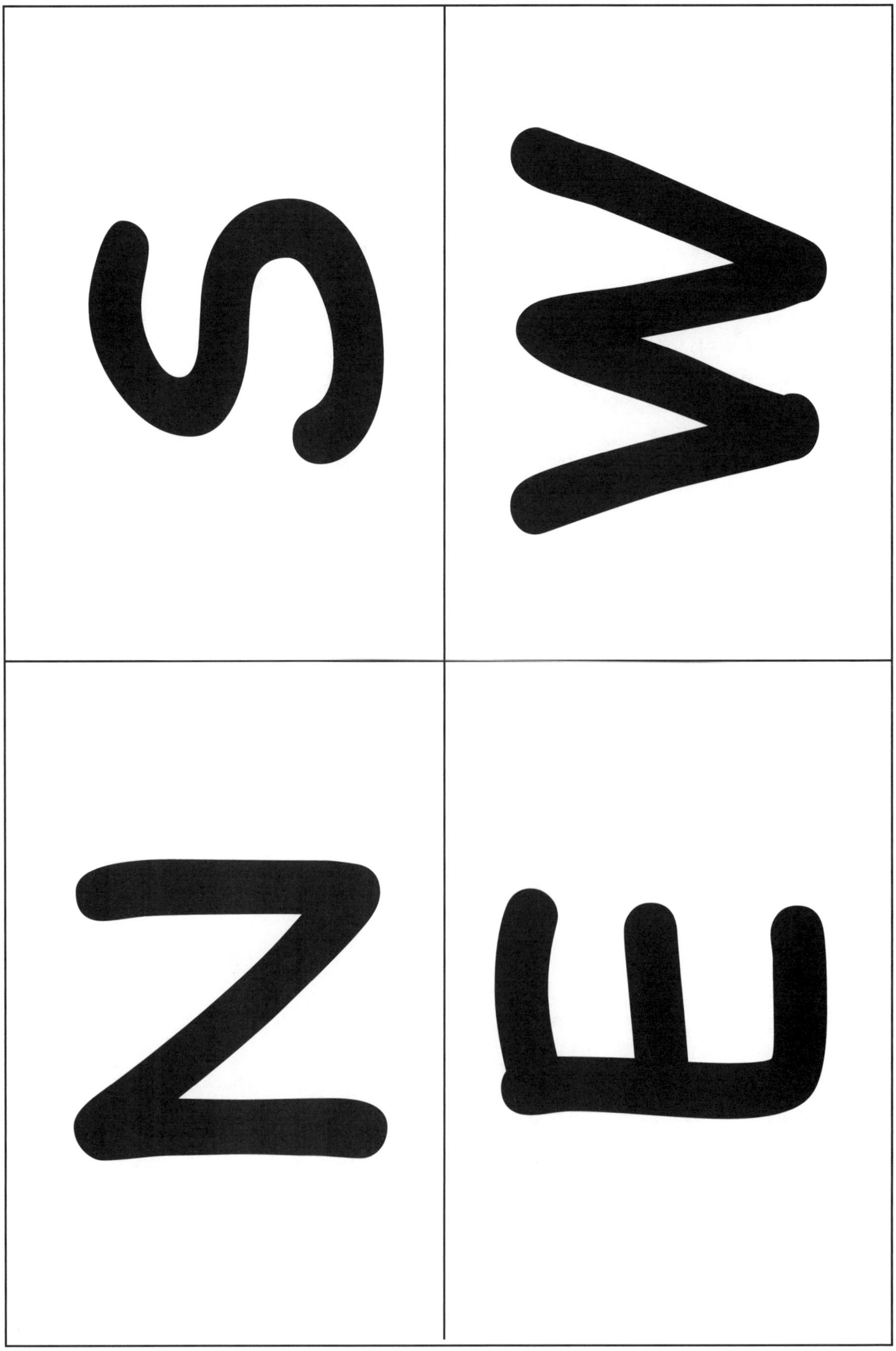

Photocopiable Sheet J

NW	SW
NE	SE

Photocopiable Sheet K

NNW	SSW
NNE	SSE

WNW	WSW
ENE	ESE

Photocopiable Sheet M

15 Making and Using 3D Shapes

Most children enjoy using and making 3D shapes. To encourage them to think more about the properties of these shapes, children should be asked to describe them (using the correct language and referring to 2D shapes). Teachers can use the following activities to give children the opportunities they need to put their knowledge into words.

Activity 1

Put a collection of 3D shapes on a table and describe each one in turn. Ask the children to locate the shape you are describing.

Activity 2

Put a collection of 3D shapes on a table and ask the children, in turn, to describe a shape. The rest of the children try to locate the correct shape.

Activity 3

Sit the children in pairs, back to back. Give each member of a pair the same 3D shapes, e.g. a cube, a cuboid, a triangular-based pyramid, a square-based pyramid, a cylinder, a triangular prism. In turn, one child in each pair describes one shape to his or her partner. The partner tries to find it. If a mistake is made, the children can discuss what went wrong; was it the description or the translation of that description?

Children love making 3D shapes. To encourage accuracy they need a specific need for their shapes. I find Christmas is an ideal time to work with these shapes. Children can make nets of shapes for the following uses. The net of a 3D shape is the 2D plan that can be folded to make the 3D shape, e.g. net of a cube could look like this:

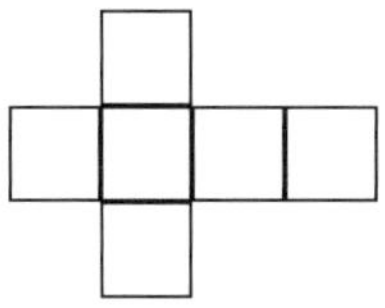

Activity 4

3D shapes make great Christmas decorations. Use shiny paper, glitter, Christmas pictures and wrapping paper to make attractive shapes for the classroom or home.

Activity 5

Make boxes for presents, using the above ideas. Emphasise the need for accuracy, as the edges of boxes need to fit properly if the present is to stay in!

Activity 6

Make Christmas trees by making pyramids and placing one on top of the other, making a hole in the bottom of each one for the next pyramid to poke through. Make a container with the net of a cube. Make the trunk with a cylinder or a cuboid.

Activity 7

Angels can be made with pyramids for the body and spheres (ping-pong balls) for the head. Be inventive with the wings.

Activity 8

Father Christmas can be made with a cylinder for his body, smaller cylinders for his legs and arms. Use a ping-pong ball (sphere) for his head. Again, a bit of invention is needed for feet and hands. With a bit of fiddling you can make boots out of cuboids.

All of these Christmas suggestions lend themselves to other topics. The children can make robots, tents, Egyptian pyramids, castles – the list could go on.

This is a topic in maths which can be covered in many areas of the curriculum, at different levels of ability, and where children are able to use their own ideas. The opportunities to develop the language of shape are tremendous.

RESOURCES

- 3D shapes
- Card
- Scissors
- Decorations (e.g. shiny paper, glitter, Christmas pictures and wrapping paper)
- Ping-pong balls
- Sellotape
- Blu-Tack

16 Coordinates

This is an area in maths which some of our children have no difficulty in understanding. Others are confused by the lines and find it difficult to remember the conventions of reading coordinates and plotting them.

It is important that the subject is introduced through familiar examples, for example through looking at maps and plans.

Dyspraxic children may need help to construct their own grids, labelling spaces and lines correctly.

Children can be given instructions to draw geometric shapes. They can be given instructions to draw 'strange' shapes. They can reflect their shapes.

The following pages give ideas of how teachers can ensure that the children have fun while using coordinates.

Activity 1

- Present a picture of a grid with coordinates marked. Discuss where children have seen such grids in their everyday life. They may think of the street A to Z, an atlas or a game.
- Discuss the language associated with the use of coordinates: axis, axes, x axis, y axis, lines, squares, boxes, north, south, east, west.
- Explain how the axes are used to describe a position – x (horizontal) before y (vertical) – and conduct a class activity to ensure that children can refer to a particular point on a grid, using the axes in the correct order.
- Explain that the lines or the spaces of the grid can be numbered or lettered. Think of times when each type of labelling would be most appropriate.
- The teacher should prepare a grid, with the x axis marked with letters and the y with numbers, naming the squares and not the lines (as on the A to Z). Choose a message and spell it out, letter by letter, on the grid, placing the letters in a random order. Fill in the remaining spaces, as in a crossword. Write a coded message. Write down the coordinates in the correct order to find the letters in the message. (See Photocopiable Sheet N for an example of this.)
- Teachers prepare a similar exercise, this time naming the lines. (See Photocopiable Sheet O.)

Find the Message (1)

8	G	Z	Q	A	Y	C	O	B
7	T	N	T	K	A	L	D	W
6	S	Y	?	Y	S	W	N	E
5	G	V	H	C	R	E	W	I
4	S	B	X	Z	N	B	I	P
3	F	M	I	N	R	M	O	D
2	U	A	J	S	V	C	X	J
1	R	F	L	E	K	F	Z	H
	A	B	C	D	E	F	G	H

Follow these directions to find the message:

D5, E7, G6, B6, G8, A2, B1, G4, E4, G7, C7, H1, C3, A4, F3, H6, E6, A6, D8, A8, D1, C6

Find the Message (2)

7	T	B	E	M	F	G	Z
6	K	D	L	O	R	E	E
5	G	N	H	T	E	I	J
4	P	P	E	R	O	X	E
3	E	Y	A	A	H	F	K
2	D	S	V	S	S	U	S
1	F	M	G	I	W	N	L
	A	B	C	D	E	F	G

Follow these directions to find the message:

C5, G6, C6, A4, F3, D1, F1, A2, C3, D7, G4, G2, B2, D3, A5, E5

Activity 1

Ask the children to construct their own grids, mark the axes as above (choosing to name lines or squares), and write a message for someone else to read, giving the coordinates in the correct order.

Activity 2

Ask the children to construct their own grid, using letters on the x axis and the numbers on the y axis. Letters and numbers are to refer to the spaces and not the lines so that the coordinates will refer to a square and not the point where two lines cross. Ask the children to draw an island with features marked (e.g. a lake, a hill, trees, a camp). Ask them to decide where the treasure is hidden and then plot a route to the treasure, using coordinates. Ask a friend to try to find the treasure, using the directions. (See Photocopiable Sheet P for a worksheet.)

Activity 3

Give the children a grid, marking lines A to H on the x axis and 1 to 8 on the y axis. Ask the children to use a ruler to draw a picture using straight lines. Each line drawn must start and end where two grid lines cross. Write out the coordinates that must be followed to reproduce their picture. The teacher should ask the children to try to follow someone else's directions on an empty grid with the same x axis and y axis markings in order to reproduce the picture. Compare the original plan with the result. Discuss the results. (See Photocopiable Sheet Q for instruction sheet.)

The cooperation involved in this exercise helps the children to understand the importance of accuracy. They can see that maths is a discipline where you can have fun but where rules need to be obeyed. Maths is a powerful language and a powerful tool and the children are being taught and trained to use it well.

RESOURCES

- Photocopiable Sheets P–Q

Treasure Island

1. Draw in the axes and write the letters (A, B, etc.) in the spaces along the bottom (the *x*-axis) and the numbers (1, 2, etc.) in the spaces up the side (the *y*-axis).

2. Draw your treasure island and put in the features (trees, sand-dunes, sand, hills and so on).

3. Decide where your treasure is to be hidden and write the coordinates for this spot on a piece of paper – then hide the paper where no one else can get at it.

4. Write instructions, giving the coordinates of the route that must be taken to reach the spot where your treasure is to be found. Do not go in one straight line. Start on the beach and make your route cover several sections of your map. Write down these instructions at the side of your map.

5. Swap your map with someone else's. See which of you can find his or her partner's treasure first. If either of you arrive in the wrong place discuss with your partner what went wrong.

Make sure that your map is well drawn and attractive. The coordinates should be accurately drawn. The letters and numbers should be correctly formed.

Draw a Picture

1. Look at your grid. The *x*-axis is marked with letters and the *y*-axis with numbers. Look at where the lines cross. Can you give a reference for these points?

2. Draw a picture using straight lines. It can be anything you like – a robot, a pattern, a plan of a room.

3. Make a note of all the coordinates needed for someone else to draw your picture. Do not forget to say where lines have to be drawn (for example, from A3 to D8) and where a new part of your picture begins.

4. Swap your instructions with a friend and ask him or her to draw your picture. You will draw your friend's.

5. Compare your pictures. You should have reproduced your friend's picture and your friend should have reproduced yours. The children should then ask the following questions:

    1. Do the pictures look exactly the same?
    2. Does the top line match on both pictures?
    3. Does the bottom line match on both papers?
    4. Do they both cover the same number of squares from top to bottom?
    5. If you put one on top of the other and hold them up to a window, do they match exactly?

6. If the pictures do not match, you can work together to find out what went wrong.

7. Try this again, drawing a different picture.